# THE WORLD OF ENERGY

## Understanding
# WATER
## POWER

## POLLY GOODMAN

**Gareth Stevens**
Publishing

Please visit our Web site, www.garethstevens.com. For a free color catalog of all our high-quality books, call toll free 1-800-542-2595 or fax 1-877-542-2596.

Library of Congress Cataloging-in-Publication Data

Goodman, Polly.
Understanding water power / Polly Goodman.
    p. cm. — (The world of energy)
Includes index.
ISBN 978-1-4339-4130-6 (library binding)
1.  Water-power—Juvenile literature.  I. Title.
TC147.G58 2011
621.2'0422—dc22
                            2010015849

This edition first published in 2011 by
**Gareth Stevens Publishing**
111 East 14th Street, Suite 349
New York, NY 10003

Editorial Director: Kerri O'Donnell
Art Director: Haley Harasymiw

Photo Credits:
AEA Technology: 22, 30, 34, 38–39; Bruce Coleman Ltd. (Goldon Langsbury) 35; Corbis: 45 (Ron Dahlquist); Ecoscene: 8–9 (Andrew Brown), 10 (Chris Knapton), 12–13 (Erik Shaffer), 13 (Andrew Brown), 14–15 (Richard Glover), 26 (Joan Creed), 32 (Rob Nichol), 36 (Nick Hawkes), 40 (M.Jones); Mary Evans Picture Library: 17, 19 (both), 20; Eye Ubiquitous: 7 (NASA), 16–17 (Brian Pickering), 43 (Davy Bold); Frank Lane Picture Agency/McCutcheon, Alaska: 42–43; Olë Steen Hansen, Denmark: 5; iStockphoto.com: cover and 1; Kvaernar Brug, Norway: 32 (both); Lionheart Books: 6–7; OPT: 31; Pelamis Wave Power Limited: 30; Samfoto: pages 28–29 (Jon Arne Sieter), 29 (Morten Loberg); Shutterstock.com: 41 (Foto011); The Stockmarket: 9, 20–21 (Ballantyne), 25 (Rose). U.S. Department of Energy: 4–5.

Printed in China
CPSIA compliance information: Batch #WAS10GS: For further information contact Gareth Stevens, New York, New York at 1-800-542-2595.

# CONTENTS

# WHAT IS WATER POWER?

Water power is a source of energy. It can be used to run machines and make electricity. Water power is a clean source of energy that is renewable, which means that it can be used again and again.

*A dam on the Columbia River, in the Pacific Northwest, is used to produce electricity.* ▼

Water power has been used for thousands of years. In the nineteenth century, steam power took over from water power. Then in the twentieth century, fossil fuels took over as the main source of energy.

Now water power is being used again. Fossil fuels are running out and, in any case, they pollute the environment with harmful waste. Scientists and engineers are looking for ways to use water power instead of fossil fuels.

▲ *A old type of waterwheel in Denmark that is used to grind grain to make flour.*

## FACT FILE

About 24 percent of electricity used in the world is generated by water power. Almost all of it is made by hydroelectric power plants.

▲ *Niagara Falls is on the border between the U.S.A. and Canada. The Falls are used to make electricity—enough for a large city.*

## The Water Cycle

Water covers three-quarters of the Earth's surface. It constantly moves between the oceans, rivers, and clouds in a natural cycle, called the water cycle.

The sun heats the water in oceans and rivers. The water evaporates and rises up into the atmosphere. When winds carry the wet air to cooler areas, it condenses and forms tiny water droplets. The water droplets form clouds.

Then the water in clouds falls as rain. The water flows down to the rivers, lakes, and oceans, and the cycle begins again.

*This diagram shows the path of water in the water cycle.* ▶

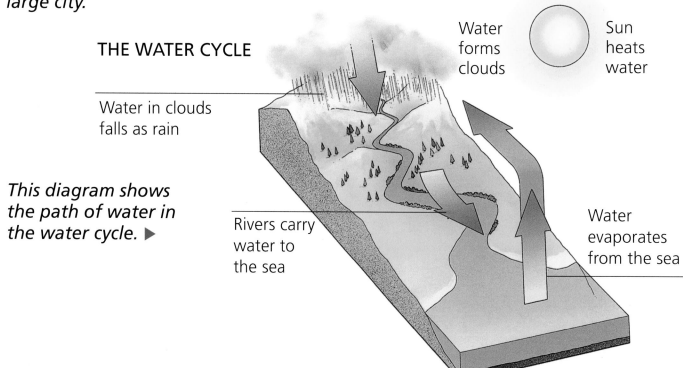

THE WATER CYCLE

Water in clouds falls as rain

Water forms clouds

Sun heats water

Rivers carry water to the sea

Water evaporates from the sea

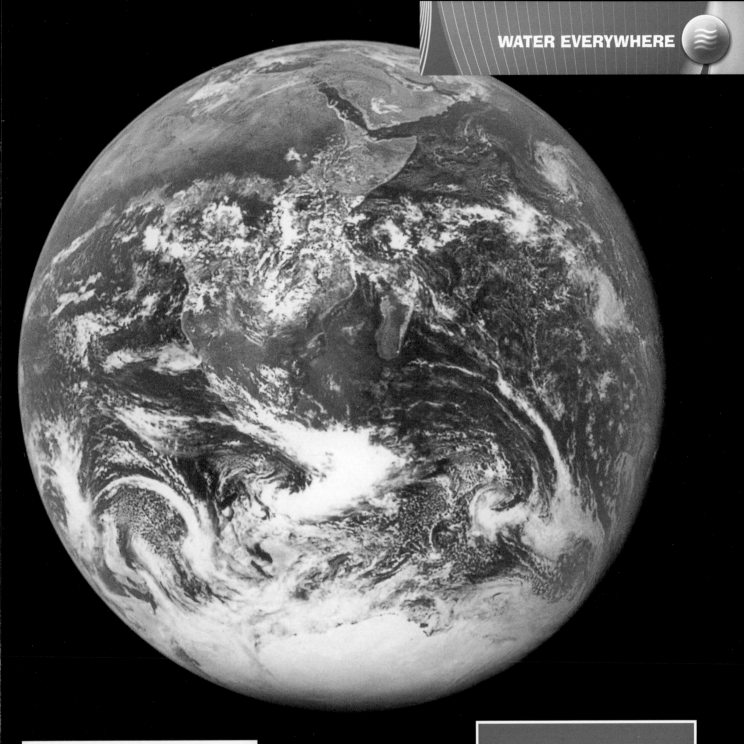

▲ *The Earth from space. The Earth is the only planet in the solar system that has oceans and rivers.*

# FACT FILE

Plants are part of the water cycle. Their roots pull up water from the soil to their leaves. It evaporates from their leaves into the Earth's atmosphere.

## Plants and Animals

All living things need water to survive. The driest places in the world have the fewest plants and animals.

Green plants make their food by mixing water with nutrients in the soil and carbon dioxide. All animals rely on plants for food. They either eat plants themselves, or they eat other animals that eat plants.

*Plants grow only where they find water. In Israel's Negev Desert, plants grow along the edge of a stream.* ▼

## FACT FILE

Only 3 percent of the world's water is fresh. The rest is salty. Most fresh water is frozen in ice caps and glaciers. This means we can use only 1 percent of the world's water, from rivers, lakes, and under the ground.

## People and Water

Over half our body weight is water. We constantly lose water every day through sweating, breathing, and going to the bathroom. So we need to replace 0.6 gallon (2.5 L) through drinking and eating.

We also use water for washing and cooking. Farmers use it to irrigate their crops, and factories use tons of water every day.

▲ *Water always flows downhill because of gravity. Pressure from pumps can send it uphill.*

## Tides

The sea level rises and falls about once every 12 hours. The changes in depth are called the tides. They are mainly caused by the moon's gravity, which pulls water toward it. Seas and oceans closest to the moon have high tides.

As the moon goes around the spinning Earth, it rises later each day. This means that high tides are later each day.

The sun's gravity also pulls water toward it. So the height of the tides depends on where the sun, moon, and Earth are. When all three are lined up, the tides are highest.

## FACT FILE

Tides change the depth of water in the sea. At low tide, harbors can become mud flats. So ship captains have to know about tide times everywhere they go.

*A crescent moon rises over the Mediterranean Sea.* ▼

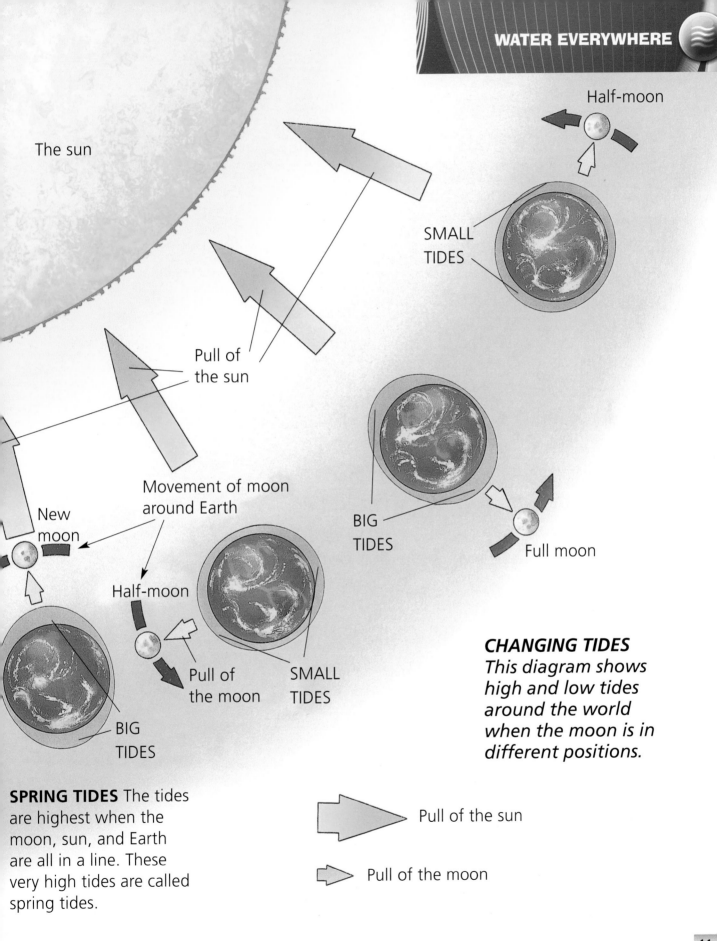

The sun

Half-moon

SMALL TIDES

Pull of the sun

Movement of moon around Earth

New moon

BIG TIDES

Full moon

Half-moon

Pull of the moon

SMALL TIDES

BIG TIDES

**CHANGING TIDES**
*This diagram shows high and low tides around the world when the moon is in different positions.*

**SPRING TIDES** The tides are highest when the moon, sun, and Earth are all in a line. These very high tides are called spring tides.

Pull of the sun

Pull of the moon

## Erosion and Flooding

Water constantly erodes, or wears away, the land. Strong waves and winds wear away coastlines. Beaches are washed away by storms, cliffs fall down, and buildings fall into the sea.

At high tides and during storms, the sea can flood the land. In the Netherlands, flood barriers called dikes were built to protect the low coastlines. In 1953, high tides broke through the dikes and 1,800 people were killed.

Not all floods are dangerous. River floods help farmers because they dump fertile mud on the land around rivers. In countries such as Bangladesh, people rely on the rivers flooding every year to keep the land fertile so they can grow crops.

*A house falls into the sea in Ireland because the cliff has been eroded by waves.* ▶

## FACT FILE

Massive waves called tsunamis are made under the sea by earthquakes. In 1868, a tsunami hit the coast of Chile. It carried a ship 2 miles (3 km) onto the land.

Waves have eroded
the softer land around
these pillars of rock
in Cornwall, UK. ▶

Monsoon rains in Indonesia. Monsoon winds collect a lot of water when they blow over warm oceans. The water falls as heavy rain. ▼

## FACT FILE

Monsoon winds change direction with the seasons. Every year, between April and October, monsoon winds blow from the Indian Ocean over India. They drop heavy rain on the way.

## Ocean Currents and Weather

Water in the oceans is constantly on the move. Bodies of water flow in certain directions around the world. These are called ocean currents. They are caused by winds and tides, and by rivers flowing into the sea.

Water also moves up and down in the oceans because water rises when it gets hotter and sinks when it gets cooler. The water's heat affects the weather. When hot water heats air above it, the hot air rises. Later, it condenses and forms clouds. Then it falls as rain.

*This map shows the path of the main ocean current. It is called the Great Ocean Conveyor Belt. It continually moves all around the world, from pole to pole.* ▶

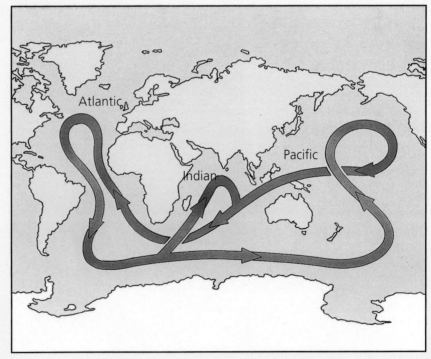

■ Warm-water currents
■ Cold-water currents

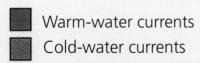

15

## Waterwheels

Waterwheels were the first machines to use water power. They were probably first used by the ancient Egyptians on the Nile River, about 4,000 years ago.

By the year 27 BCE, they were in everyday use by the Romans. Most waterwheels were used to grind flour, using millstones. Some worked hammers or bellows in forges.

**FACT FILE**

By the sixth century CE, mills driven by waterwheels were used throughout Europe and the Middle East. Growing cities depended on water power to help feed their people. In 1086, there were 5,624 water mills in England. This was written in the Domesday Book.

*This is an old waterwheel on the Test River, in the UK. Only a few mills with working waterwheels have survived until modern times.* ▶

*A French waterwheel in the sixteenth century. It works four bellows, which blow air into furnaces to keep them burning.* ▶

A waterwheel is a wheel with paddles around the edge. When water pushes against the paddles, they turn the wheel and the axle in the center. The axle could be fixed to millstones. Or it could be fixed to other machines through sets of links.

During the Industrial Revolution, large waterwheels were used to run machinery in factories.

17

## Tidal Mills

In the estuaries of rivers, tides flow in and out. In the 1100s, engineers found out how to use the rise and fall of the tides for energy.

Wooden gates were built across a river, close to the estuary. When the tides came in, the gates were open.

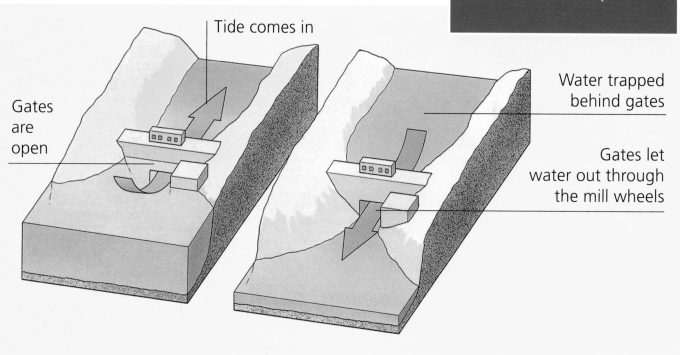

Tide comes in

Gates are open

Water trapped behind gates

Gates let water out through the mill wheels

But when the tides turned to go out, the closed gates trapped the water behind them. Once enough water had collected, it was allowed to flow back through a mill wheel. The collected water flowed much faster than normal, because it was under pressure.

*This diagram shows the parts of a windmill and waterwheel. It is from a science book called* Physics in Pictures, *published in 1882.* ▶

▲ *The diagram above shows a barge with a waterwheel. The wheel used the power of the tides to work tools.*

# Steam Engines

In the eighteenth century, steam engines were used instead of waterwheels. The steam engine also used water for power, but it heated up the water first to turn it into steam.

When water turns into steam, it expands quickly. In steam engines, the steam pushed a piston that turned a wheel. The water was heated up by burning coal in a furnace.

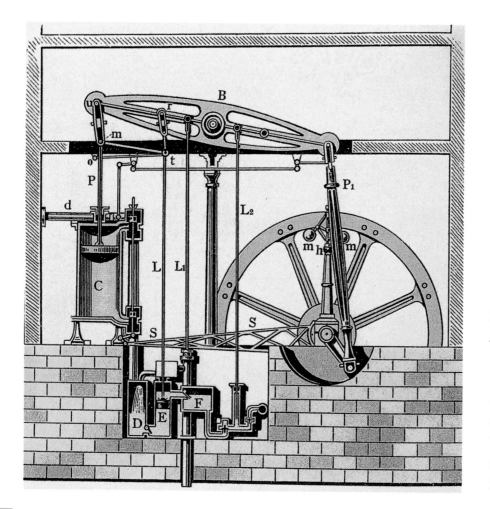

◄ *A diagram of the steam engine made by James Watt, in 1765.*

*Steam pushed a piston down. The piston turned the wheel of a machine. Then the steam was let out.* ▶

## FACT FILE

The first steam locomotive was built in Wales by Richard Trevithick, in 1804. It traveled at a speed of 9 miles (15 km) an hour.

*Steam engines started the Industrial Revolution in Europe and the United States.* ▼

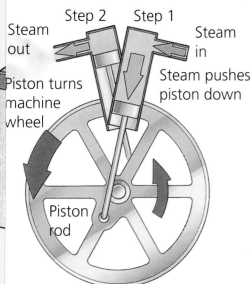

Step 2    Step 1

Steam out

Steam in

Piston turns machine wheel

Steam pushes piston down

Piston rod

The first practical steam engine was invented by Thomas Newcomen in 1712. It was made to pump water out of deep coal mines.

Then, in 1765, James Watt improved the first steam engine. He used it to drive other machines. Soon there were hundreds of steam engines driving machines in European factories.

# Hydroelectric Power

Water power is made into electricity in hydroelectric power plants. To make electricity, water flows through a turbine, making it spin. The turbine drives a generator. The generator makes electricity. This is called hydropower.

To make the turbine spin as fast as possible and make the most electricity, the water has to be put under pressure. Water pressure is greater in deeper water. So deep reservoirs are made at hydroelectric power plants by building a dam across a river.

The water that flows through the turbine comes from the bottom of the reservoir. It is under the greatest pressure.

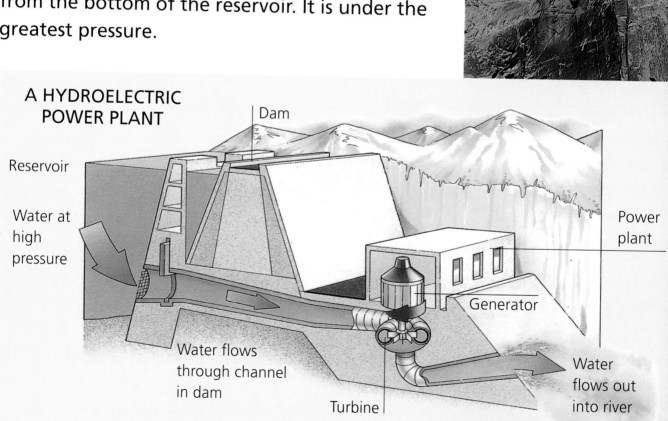

## A HYDROELECTRIC POWER PLANT

Dam

Reservoir

Water at high pressure

Water flows through channel in dam

Turbine

Generator

Power plant

Water flows out into river

*The Glen Canyon Dam across the Colorado River in Arizona. The reservoir crosses the border between Arizona and Utah. ▼*

# FACT FILE

Hydroelectric power plants make about one-fourth of the world's electricity. The most powerful hydroelectric power plant is the Three Gorges Dam complex on the Yangtze River in Hubei, China. It makes enough power for several provinces and cities.

## Pumped-Storage Power Plants

The need for electricity changes every minute. More electricity is needed during the day, when people are awake, than at night. So power plants constantly have to adjust the amount of electricity they supply.

Pumped-storage power plants can store energy. They use two reservoirs. At night, when the need for electricity is low, water is pumped uphill from a lower reservoir to an upper reservoir.

During the day, if there is a need for more electricity, the water from the upper reservoir can be quickly used to make electricity. It falls to the lower reservoir through the turbines.

*A hydroelectric power plant in Brazil. The pipes in the front of the photograph carry water uphill, where it is stored in an upper reservoir.* ▼

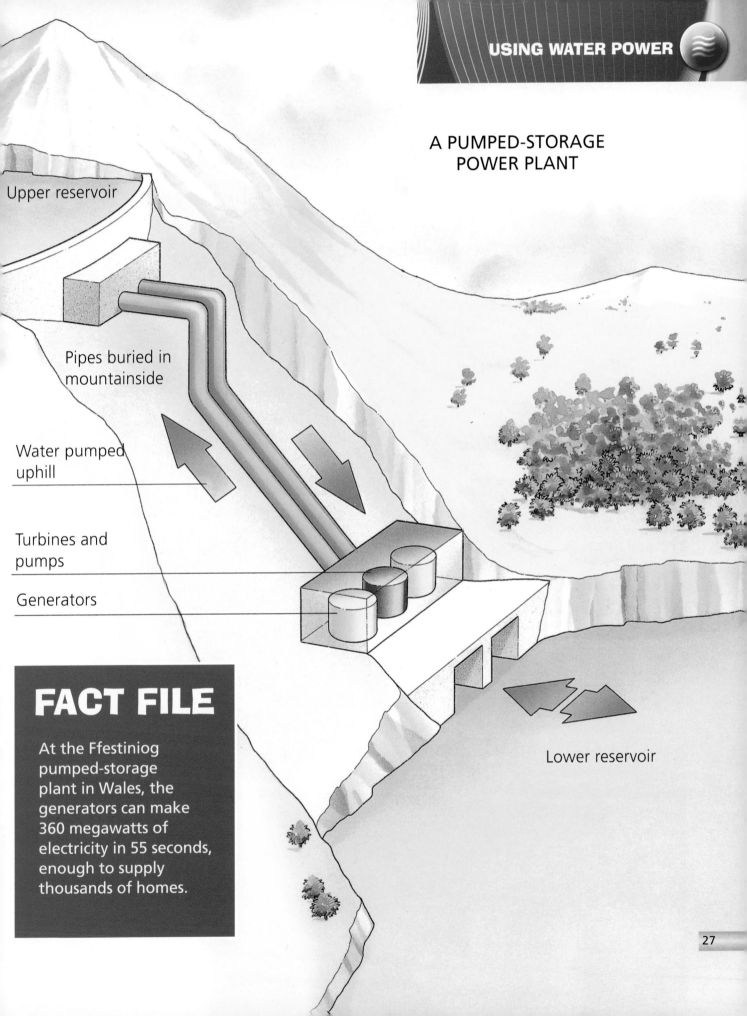

A PUMPED-STORAGE
POWER PLANT

Upper reservoir

Pipes buried in
mountainside

Water pumped
uphill

Turbines and
pumps

Generators

Lower reservoir

# FACT FILE

At the Ffestiniog
pumped-storage
plant in Wales, the
generators can make
360 megawatts of
electricity in 55 seconds,
enough to supply
thousands of homes.

People in Norway use more electricity per person than in any other country. Most electricity is used for heating and lighting.

Over 99 percent of Norway's electricity is made from water power. Instead of building coal or oil-fired power plants, they built hydroelectric power plants instead. The high mountains and heavy rainfall in Norway are ideal for making hydroelectric power.

## FACT FILE

Each person in Norway uses about 30,000 kilowatt-hours of electricity a year. In Denmark each person uses about 6,000 kilowatt-hours, and in Switzerland they use only 800 kilowatt-hours each.

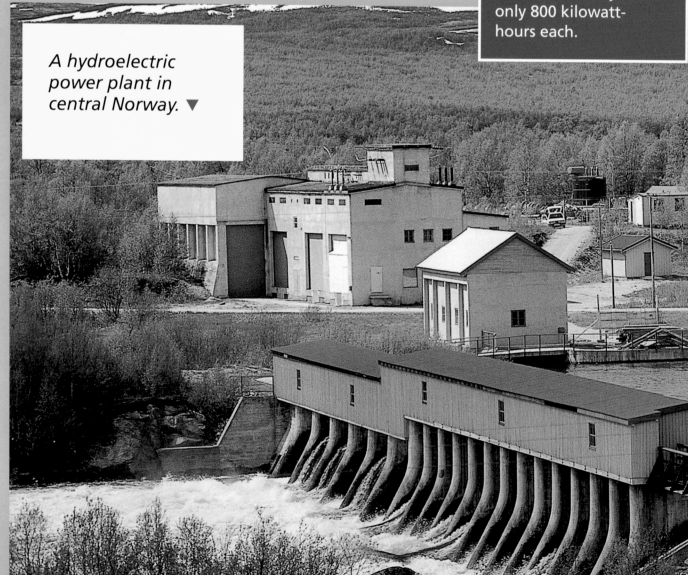

*A hydroelectric power plant in central Norway.* ▼

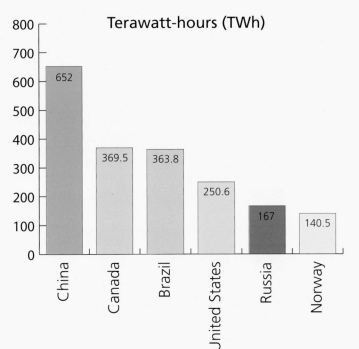

*This chart shows the six countries that made the most hydroelectricity in 2009. One terawatt hour is a million million watt hours.* ▼

**Terawatt-hours (TWh)**

| Country | TWh |
|---|---|
| China | 652 |
| Canada | 369.5 |
| Brazil | 363.8 |
| United States | 250.6 |
| Russia | 167 |
| Norway | 140.5 |

▲ *The generator room at a power station in Norway.*

No other country makes as much of its electricity from water power as Norway. Electricity in Norway is cheap and clean. The only fuel that is burned at a hydroelectric power plant is in the machines that built it. This means that the energy used in Norway does less damage to the environment than energy used in countries nearby.

## Electricity from Waves

The wind whips up the surface of the sea into waves and blows them toward the land. As each wave rolls over the sea, the water level goes up and down. This movement can be used to make electricity using a wave energy converter.

In a wave energy converter, a float on the water's surface bobs up and down. It changes the up-and-down movement into a spinning movement. The spin drives an electricity generator. The electricity is then sent to shore by an underwater cable.

*A wave farm off the coast of Portugal uses Pelamis wave energy converters to generate electricity.* ▼

## Wave Energy Converter

The PowerBuoy® is a new wave energy converter that bobs and up and down with the ocean waves to drive a generator. Each PowerBuoy® can make 150 kilowatts of electricity without burning fossil fuels that produce carbon dioxide (a gas that adds to air pollution).

A PowerBuoy® wave farm is being developed 2.5 miles (4 km) off the coast of Reedsport, Oregon. The wave farm will have ten PowerBuoy® units that can generate enough electricity for 375 homes. It will prevent around 2,000 tons of carbon dioxide from entering the atmosphere each year.

▲ *A PowerBuoy® wave converter is tested off the island of Ohau, Hawaii. Most of the unit is under the water*

One machine that uses the power of waves is called an oscillating water column generator. It is a vertical pipe fixed to a cliff face, with an open top and bottom.

Trial plants using the oscillating water column generator have been built in Norway, Japan, and the UK. Inside the pipe, there is a turbine linked to an electricity generator.

*Waves force water through a natural blowhole.* ▼

When waves reach the cliff, the water level inside the pipe rises and falls. Air rushes up and down the pipe, making the turbine spin. The turbine drives the electricity generator.

The only water column generators that have been made so far have been destroyed by battering waves. Engineers are trying to improve its design, and find other ways of using the power of waves.

▲ *A water column generator in Norway.*

*This shows the inside of an oscillating water column generator. The blades of the turbine are red.* ▼

## FACT FILE

The oscillating water column generator was first made in the early 1980s. It was invented by student engineers from Northern Ireland and a Norwegian company in Oslo.

The biggest tidal power plant in the world is on the Rance River, in France. It was built in 1966 and makes enough electricity for a quarter of a million homes.

The power plant's barrier stretches 2,460 feet (750 m) across the river, and the water passes through 24 tunnels. Each tunnel has a turbine and a generator in it.

## FACT FILE

In the estuary of the Rance River, the difference in height between high and low tide can be 44 feet (13.5 m).

▲ *The barrage across the Rance River is also a road.*

CUTAWAY DIAGRAM OF
THE TIDAL BARRAGE
ON THE RIVER RANCE

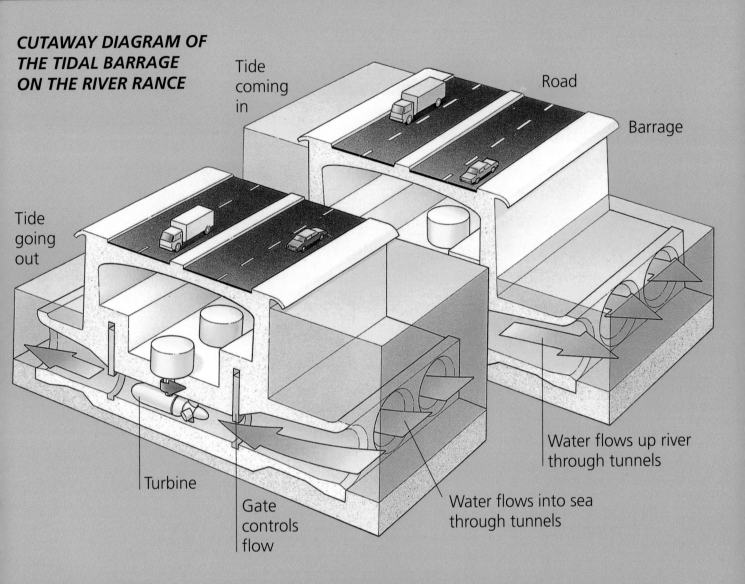

Tide coming in

Road

Barrage

Tide going out

Turbine

Gate controls flow

Water flows into sea through tunnels

Water flows up river through tunnels

▲ The tidal barrage across the Rance River is an important transportation route, as well as an electricity generator.

In most tidal power plants, the incoming tide is too slow to turn the turbines.

The Rance River meets the sea in a bay. This funnels the tides coming from the Atlantic up the river mouth. This means the incoming tides are more powerful than most rivers. So the turbines in the power plant are driven by the incoming and the outgoing tides.

Steam turbines are the most powerful type of machinery driven by water today. Like steam engines, steam turbines use the force made when water turns into steam and expands quickly. But they work better than steam engines, because they immediately make a spinning movement instead of using a set of links.

The force of the steam pushes the blades of a turbine inside an airtight case. The turbine blades turn a shaft. The shaft is linked to an electricity generator.

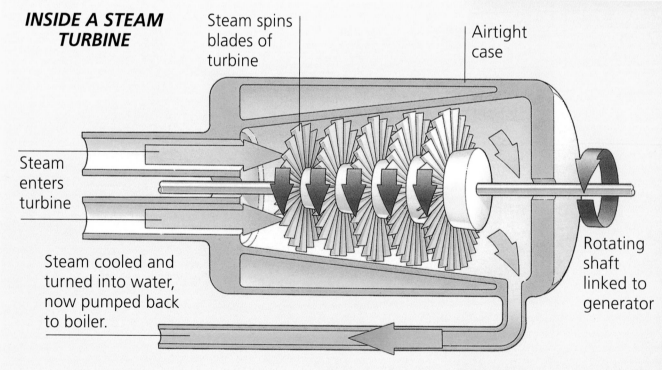

**INSIDE A STEAM TURBINE**

Steam spins blades of turbine

Airtight case

Steam enters turbine

Steam cooled and turned into water, now pumped back to boiler.

Rotating shaft linked to generator

# FACT FILE

Simple steam turbines use the force of steam on the turbine blades. Other turbines use the speed of the steam as it expands. These turbines have two sets of blades, which the steam rushes through at high speed.

*Pairs of steam turbines and generators, fed by steam pipes, inside a nuclear power plant.* ▼

## Water-Jet Engines

Water-jet engines propel boats along by pumping out a high-speed jet of water. Water is sucked in at the front of the boat. It is passed through a set of high-pressure pumps.

The pumps push the water into a narrow, fast jet. The jet shoots out of the back of the boat, propelling it along.

▲ *The Boeing Jetfoil is a hydrofoil with waterjet engines.*

**FACT FILE**

Scallops are a type of shellfish that use natural jet propulsion to move through the water. They squirt out a jet of water by snapping their shells shut.

Car ferries, high-speed boats, and sports craft use water-jet engines. Because they do not have propellers, they have fewer problems with shallow water, weeds, or ropes.

Water-jet engines are the same as the ones used by fighter-planes. But instead of making a jet of air, they pump out a jet of water.

*A jet-ski uses a water-jet engine to propel it across the water.* ▼

*A ferry such as a SeaCat uses water jets to help it move.* ▼

Pumps

Water jet out

Water in

*Water jets in Alaska wash out gravels that may contain gold.* ▼

## FACT FILE

Hoses have been used in mining for over a hundred years. But using water jets to cut through materials was only invented in 1968, by Norman Franz, in the United States.

## Water-Jet Tools

When water is pushed into a jet under pressure, it can clean materials by blasting off the dirt. At a higher pressure, it can even cut through hard materials such as rock.

Water is put under pressure using a machine called a compressor. It is sprayed out through a hose, with a nozzle that pushes it into a jet.

Water jets are used in mining. They cut through the earth to find minerals. Then they wash the minerals into an area where they can be collected. Water jets are also used to clean buildings that have been blackened by air pollution.

*A water-jet tool is used to clean a building.* ▼

Many countries want to make their energy from cleaner, renewable energy sources. Hydroelectric power, or hydropower, has the potential to generate half of the world's electricity. In 2010, hydropower produced 6 percent of all electricity in the United States. This number is set to rise with new research and water power developments.

## FACT FILE

A machine called an Ocean Thermal Energy Converter is being developed to make electricity in tropical seas. It uses the difference in temperature between different depths of water to drive a turbine.

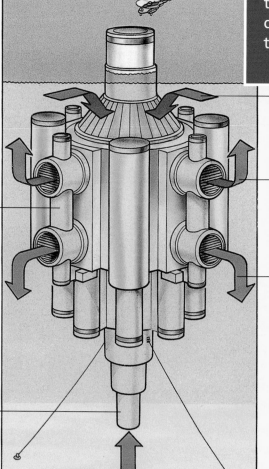

*The Ocean Thermal Energy Converter uses warm water to change a liquid into a gas. The gas drives a turbine.* ▶

Warm water goes in

Warm water comes out and rises

Cold water comes out and sinks

Turbine

Cold water rises into the machine and cools the gas

Big water power projects are being planned across the world. South Korea is building a tidal power plant that may become the world's largest. It will have 300 tidal turbines, which will work like windmills in the water. Each turbine will be 66 feet (20 m) high. The plant should produce 300 megawatts of electricity—enough to power 200,000 homes.

Smaller projects are being developed, too. A company called Rentricity has invented a small turbine that uses the power of flushing toilets to create electricity in the home! There are many ways to use water power as a practical source of energy for the future.

*The vast power of waves may provide our energy for the future.* ▼

45

# GLOSSARY

**Axle** A rod that a wheel is attached to.

**Bellows** A pair of airbags with handles used for blowing air into a fire.

**Blowhole** A hole in rocks or a tunnel through which air, smoke, or water can escape.

**Cargo** The load of goods carried by a ship or an aircraft.

**Condenses** Changes from a gas into a liquid by cooling.

**Currents** Bodies of water moving in a certain direction.

**Domesday Book** The record of the lands of England made in 1086 by order of William I.

**Engineers** People who design and build things such as machines and bridges.

**Erosion** The wearing away of something, such as land.

**Estuary** A broad mouth of a river, where tides flow in and out.

**Evaporates** Turns into a gas from a liquid or solid.

**Expand** To get bigger.

**Forges** Workshops where metals were heated and shaped.

**Fossil fuels** Coal, oil, and natural gas formed from the remains of plants and animals over millions of years.

**Furnace** A container for a very hot fire.

**Generator** A machine that changes movement energy into electricity.

**Glacier** A large mass of ice that moves very slowly down a mountain or valley.

**Gravity** The force that attracts objects toward the center of Earth.

**Habitats** Natural homes of plants and animals.

**Horizontal** Parallel to the horizon.

**Hydroelectric** Energy made from the power of fast-flowing water.

**Irrigation** The supply of water to land.

**Kilowatt-hours (kWh)** A unit of energy that is equal to 1,000 watts of electrical power being used for one hour.

**Megawatt (MW)** A unit of energy that equals one million watts.

**Millstones** A pair of rounded, flat stones used for grinding corn, wheat, or other grain.

**Propel** To drive or push forward. Propulsion is the act of driving something forward.

**Renewable** Something that can be replaced.

**Reservoir** A place where water is collected and stored.

**Rotating** Turning around a center, such as a shaft.

**Shaft** A bar that helps parts of a machine turn.

**Turbines** Angled blades fitted to a shaft that are made to rotate by the force of water, steam, or air.

**Vertical** Straight up and down.

**Wave energy converter** A device that makes electricity from waves using floats and electricity generators.

# FURTHER INFORMATION

## Further Reading

*Energy Today: Geothermal Energy*
by Alan Watchel
Chelsea House Publications, 2010

*Geothermal Energy: Using Earth's Furnace*
by Carrie Gleason
Crabtree Publishing Company, 2008

*Powering the Future: New Energy Technologies*
by Eva Thaddeus
University of New Mexico Press, 2010

## Web Sites

http://home.clara.net/darvill/altenerg/geothermal.htm

http://science.howstuffworks.com/geothermal-energy.htm

http://www.geothermal.org/what.html

*ENERGY CONSUMPTION*
*The use of energy is measured in joules per second, or watts. Different machines use up different amounts of energy. The diagram on the right gives a few examples.* ▶

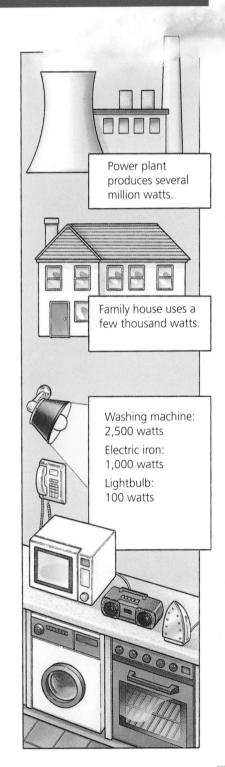

Power plant produces several million watts.

Family house uses a few thousand watts.

Washing machine: 2,500 watts
Electric iron: 1,000 watts
Lightbulb: 100 watts

# INDEX